Foreword by Barbara Morris-Blake

SUZEN FROMSTEIN
SUITS AND
LADDERS

**Ten proven ways to keep your job safe
(with a few jokes thrown in)**

**Based on the combined wisdom of 102
real people with real jobs**

CAREER/SELF HELP/EDUCATION/BUSINESS/GENERAL

SUITS AND LADDERS *by Suzen Fromstein*
Ten Proven Ways To Keep Your Job Safe (with a few jokes thrown in)
Based on the combined wisdom of 102 real people with real jobs

ISBN: 978-0-9881515-2-9
The Write Connections Inc.
suzen@suzenfromstein.com
416-471-3845

Also by Suzen Fromstein

Want To Inform, Influence And Entertain Like A Pro?
Simply Recognize The Seven Deadly Sins Of
Public Speaking And Then Avoid Them

Killers, Coffins & Cadavers
A humorous guide to death and dying

To my parents, Aaron and Bea Fromstein
who encouraged me to learn from my mistakes.
And to my sons, Mikel and Dustin Fromstein,
who continue to love me in spite of them.

Some early Amazon reviews

From Barb Amsden, August 16, 2013, amazon.com: Suits and Ladders is a small, easy-to-read book with big ideas on how to manage in the hard corporate world. While giving helpful hints on how to play the game without completely losing your soul, it's a book to read with your e-reader's annotation feature at the ready (or with a highlighter in the physical world) for a quick reminder again and again of key lessons for you. For parents, it's a great gift for the teenager and 20-somethings you want off the couch and earning their keep (with some humor to keep them reading 'til the last page). It's a must-read for managers too... or at least managers who want to build effective teams. And its common-sense tips can even be used to improve relationships with friends and family. Try it - you'll like it!

From Flipper, August 13, 2013, amazon.com: Very good a must get book for anyone in the working world. This has to be one of the best books on this subject.

From Rick Ogrodzinski, August 7, 2013, amazon.ca: Every chapter needs no explanation. It's what we successful veterans do and have done during our careers. The younger generations need to learn; Suits and Ladders teaches the fundamental principles and practices. This book is a 'must read'. Congratulations on a real winner Suzen!

From Pat, July 30, 2013, amazon.com: Suits and Ladders is a slim, handy-sized volume and the kind of book that I can just pop in my handbag, and open up on any page when I have a few minutes to spare during my busy workweek. The advice and scenarios are realistic, and are drawn from successful managers who may not be household names, but who have been able to navigate their way in the corporate world –

something not everybody can do very well. Not only is the advice sound, but also the tone is also very down-to-earth. I didn't get the impression that the author or her sources were pontificating. Instead, it's about sharing good, sound principles that I can use as I deal with my own forays in today's corporate world. It's also an easy read, and is very well structured. Suzen Fromstein offers ten survival strategies. Each survival strategy is structured and explained from the outset, offering excellent pieces of advice in digestible formats with what she calls "Takeaways" at the end of each section of the survival guide. I just had a bit of a disagreement with my boss on a particular issue at work. I was told, "Just go with the boss." I followed this advice, which was very well explained on page 50. So, I feel that the content is very relevant to my current professional situation. There is also something to be said for reading a survival guide for the corporate world that also injects some much-needed humor. After all, are we not supposed to work so we can live? So that was another element that I found really pleasing when reading this book. I would recommend this book to anybody who is serious about getting ahead in his or her job, and who doesn't want to read a long, lengthy tome. It is tiny but mighty.

From Marcia Ross, July 3, 2013, amazon.ca: What do you really have to do to hold your corporate job? For a start, read Suits and Ladders. It's a quick, well-written, enjoyable read that packs a punch. By combining the hard-earned knowledge of senior executives with a number of case studies, the book provides many actionable insights and insider tips on what you need to do to keep your corporate gig. Plus move up. Suits and Ladders is not only worth a first read, it's worth a re-read every year or two. Just as the job world changes and evolves, so do individuals. Which means that the advice you missed in your last read might well sneak up and smack you in the head a couple of years later in a re-read ... advantageously, of course.

From Florence, July 1, 2013, amazon.ca: They say you can't teach common sense...well, here it is, a great little book of wisdom and common sense to help you along your career path. We can easily fall into the trap of trying to keep up with technology, new skills, new processes to stay ahead, but a lot of what we really need are proven strategies and common sense things you may not find all in one great little book. This is a quick read and a great resource for anyone in the workplace. I'm going to recommend it to junior PR practitioners as a must read.

From Lana, Jun 21 2013, amazon.ca: What I liked the most about Suzen Fromstein's book *Suits and Ladders: Ten Proven Ways to Keep Your Job Safe* is the realism and common sense. It's a refreshing change from traditional motivational read. The book does not contain unrealistic motivation, but rather very practical easily applicable ideas. The book is a reminder of real life situations in the corporate world, that put in new perspective my own job search and perception of my career. I found a few eye-opening ideas, and a reminder that collaboration in today's workforce is as important as, if not more important than, the hard technical skills. Suzen puts a lot of things in perspective, such as – realistic timelines, winning attitudes and turning around downers into cushions. I thoroughly enjoyed the book as it is insightful, funny, very much to the point and also timely for someone in transition like myself.

From Andrew, July 6, 2013, amazon.ca: Got it one of those hard to fall asleep nights. While a lot of books are focusing on so called the great successors. Ok, well, what do they do in case things go south? Here is my book: they take out their golden parachute conveniently stacked in their brief case, and take-off to wait it out on the golf coarse. So if you're like me and not into sky-diving, this book is for us and about us, the real working people who do their work.

From Susan Yellin, July 2, 2013, amazon.com: The book may be small in size but Suzen Fromstein's Suits and Ladders packs in hundreds of must-read words of advice for anyone wanting to learn how to get and keep a corporate job or those looking for a new one. The no-nonsense survival strategies are smart and easy-to-read and have been culled from the real-life careers of 102 men and women Fromstein personally interviewed (although I'm sure the clever wit is all hers). Some call it a primer, but I think even those who have kept their corporate jobs for years, or moved from one job to another over the years, can learn a thing or two.

From Melodie Campbell (Author), June 29, 2013, amazon.com: Dead on, pithy, and to the point; I thoroughly enjoyed this primer on how to survive in the corporate jungle. In fact, if I were still teaching marketing at Sheridan College, this would be required reading for my students. The architecture of the book makes it extremely easy to read. The quotes from research subjects are right on the mark and support the material well. An extremely useful and perceptive book for those currently in the jungle, and those studying to be there.

From Debbie, June 24, 2013, amazon.com: I have learned a lot from reading this book and not half-way through. It really explains how to act in the corporate world and what NOT to do that I DO! Now to apply what I have learned and become VP one day!

From JC, June 21, 2013, amazon.com: *Suits and Ladders* is more than a careers survival narrative. Yes, I said careers because we all know that before we go for the eternal dirt nap, we will experience 2 or more careers. This tome borders on a philosophical experience. Suzen Fromstein has obviously experienced much of what her 102 real people with real jobs have shared with the readers of *Suits and Ladders.* Otherwise, she could not have written what she did in a way that easily describes very complex situations in the corporate world. The book is now an accessory of my mobile office, as is The Greatest Salesman in the World by Augustine (Og) Mandino. *Suits and Ladders* and The Greatest Salesman in the World are mentors in my business world.

Marjorie Podmore, June 11, 2013, amazon.co.uk: Overall, good advice to climb the corporate ladder. Being self employed for the past 39 years or so, only part of the book I could take on board. I could understand where the author was coming from and therefore understand that it applies to a person (male or female) wishing to get on within a company or even to change positions or jobs especially when leaving Uni. A little more humor may help.

From M. Moya (The Kindle Book Review), June 5, 2013, amazon.com: This book is written in a lively, easy to understand manner. It is pragmatic, realistic, and mostly preaches common sense. The main lesson to take away, which cannot be repeated too often, is that your relations within your company or institution matter far more for your job security, than actual performance (as long as you are basically competent). One might say that most employed people already know most of what the author advises, but knowing in theory, and consistently acting on the knowledge are often different things. It can never hurt to reinforce your adaptation to corporate requirements by reading this book and pondering the good advice it contains. That said, maybe the most appropriate target group for this book would be young people looking for their first corporate jobs. On reading it, they could not fail to ask themselves if the pay is really worth submitting to all this, - always making your boss look good, keeping your head down, giving long hours to a corporation that can fire you at any moment - and if this is the sort of lifestyle they will be able to stomach for long. It may be better to think about this issue in advance, than find out the hard way that you are not cut out for the corporate environment. As a side note - when this reviewer started her own corporate career over thirty years ago, a book like this would have been hard to imagine. It shows how low we have come in our economic cycle that now it is already considered an achievement to be spared in the next round of restructuring.

From B. Cacciatore, May 28, 2013, amazon.ca: The way this book was put together had me intrigued. The business books I usually read are of a single person's success and how they got there and how you can supposedly achieve the same. This was different as it was more of an overview of what 102 successful people went through to get to where they are. Instead of being a individual how-to story, it shows the similarities of what worked and what didn't work to get to where they got in life. This set *Suits And Ladders* apart from the bulk of what is out there. Another thing that I really enjoyed about the book was the way it was written and how each chapter took a different look at digging your heels in. The research that went into the creation of the book was also well documented in a way that makes it easy to follow. When you then add in the humor of the author, it makes for a book that you don't want to put down. It is very rare that a book about business keeps my interest and has me reading the whole thing in a couple of sittings instead of over the course of weeks while reading something more captivating. While the topic could end up very dull, pretentious, and/or preachy, *Suits and Ladders* finds the perfect balance of easy to read, different points of view, and quite bit of humor making it a fun and enjoyable read. I recommend this book for anyone that is in the business world that wants to get ahead, or at the very least make sure they are safe where they are.

From Brian, May 24, 2013, amazon.ca: Be personable, be engaged, listen & learn. *Suits and Ladders* is an easy to read primer for those starting out on their career journey. Many of the survival skills outlined can help you keep your job but also help you navigate your way through tough situations and obstacles. Each strategy is listed with case studies provided. An extra bonus from the book is the additional reading recommendations given by those who were interviewed. *Suits and Ladders* is a good overview of skill sets required in today's work environment. This would be a great gift to a new graduate or someone starting their work life.

Please also see www.suzenfromstein.com for additional reviews from Al Emid, Nina Spencer and Zel Spillman

Table of Contents

Acknowledgments

I would like to thank Madhavi Acharya-Tom Yew, Victoria Amaral, Barbara Amsden, Peter Amsden, Hadley Archer, Dauna Atkins, Richard E. Austin, Patricia (Trish) Barbato, Debra Bennett, Andrew Berwick, Anu Bhalla, Philip Blackford, Lydia Boyko, Steven Braudo, Rosemary Breitenbach (Trufal), Perry Brock, Maryska Bushnell, Ozy Camacho, Josh Caplan, Jodie Carrera, Ed Cartwright, Mario Causarano, Sourav Chatterjee, Jonathan Chevreau, Michael Claener, Laurie M. Clark, Philip Clark, Janet Comeau, Danielle Cote, Jacqui d'Eon, Darin Diehl, Geraldine Dona, Maura Drew-Lytle, Pat Dunwoody, Leah Eichler, Bob Engel, Kathy Fairbarns, Len Gamache, Eric Gilboord, Jason Gourlay, Roberta Greenberg, Bob Greenhalgh, Gordon Guild, Monica Gutschi, Christine Haeberlin, Angela Haier, Ann Harris, Graeme Harris, Ranil Herath, Jess Hungate, Jordan Ivanov, Lauragaye Jackson, Judith John, Mary Kasmetis, Steve Kee, Donna Kerry, Sylvie Lachapelle, Dwarka Lakhan, Michael H. List, Rudy Luukko, Deanna MacDougal, Tony Martino, Jane Matthews, Michelle McClure, John McGuinness, Gordon K. McIvor, Mathew McTaggart, Oriana Melo, Linda Menache, Sabina Michael, Adam Muggleton, Teresa Muzzi, Philip Neukom, Rick Ogrodzinski, John Parker, Howard Pearl, Nancy Perkins, Walter Pestrak, June Pierotti, Maria Pimenta, Krys Potapczyk, Anthony Raman, Michel Resendes, Glain Roberts-McCabe, Susan Rogers, Klaus Schuller, Annie Smith, Pamela Steer, Lawrence Stevenson, Jane Stirling, Tim Stoate, Debbie Stojanovic, Danny Tam, Karen Tinsley, Richard Thomson, Paul Tsaparis, Ashok Wagadarikar, George Wamala, Mark Weseluck, John White, Dennis Yanchus and Karen Yule for your candor. I hope you are as delighted with *Suits and Ladders* as am I.

I would also like to thank my extraordinarily talented son Mikel for his cover design, print layout and eagle eye, my niece Ariel Fromstein and my friends Devin Scannura and Shirley Crockett for their editing prowess, Michael Nemiroff for his sparkling comedy edits, Donna Carrick for her e-book layout expertise, and my brother David Fromstein and my friend Elizabeth Payea Butler for their unstinting encouragement.

Foreword
by Barbara Morris-Blake

Although there are many credible business books on corporate survival, I have not come across a book quite like *Suits and Ladders*. Suzen Fromstein's corporate survival guide consolidates the actual strategies 51 men and 51 women (from a variety of industries and from several different English-speaking countries) use to keep their corporate jobs safe. She lays out the ten proven strategies in a straightforward, direct and often humorous way. The information is easy to understand and fun to read.

I have interviewed and coached over 10,000 junior-to-senior level people over the past twenty years. My articles on leadership development and personal effectiveness frequently appear in the media and I write a regular blog "Ask About Work." It's fair to say that I've seen and heard just about everything, which is why I believe *Suits and Ladders* is a must-read, regardless of age, stage or level.

It's challenging to find a great job. It's equally difficult to hang on to it. *Suits and Ladders* is the exit interview and the corporate survival coach you wish you had. This one-of-a-kind survival guide explains the strategies 102 real people with real jobs use to stay employed. Following their lead gives you a better chance of survival, or at least, gives you a fighting chance at survival. I highly recommend this important work.

Primary Research

The skinny

Research pool

Sectors/geography

Their titles

Top ten survival skills

Summary charts

The skinny

In spite of my laser intellect, bubbly personality and award-winning technical skills, I still managed to burn my way through three senior communications positions in five years.

Rather than blame the bad economy, bad politics, bad processes, bad bosses, bad luck, bad husbands, bad boyfriends, and the really bad takeout I had for dinner last night, I decided to research exactly what was required to keep my corporate job safe and then to speak and write about what I had learned.

My primary research consisted of one year's worth of conversations and personal interviews with 102 mid-to-senior level managers (51 men and 51 women), from a variety of industries and from several different English-speaking countries.

I had no set interview questions. I simply asked our 102 mentors to describe what they did to keep their corporate jobs safe. Then I consolidated their combined wisdom into this one survival guide.

If a mentor mentioned a tip or a strategy in our interview, it is included here. If not, I did not mention it. Other than four of the bonehead moves described in the Case Studies and all of the comedy, I have kept my personal opinions, biases, preferences and uncorroborated research from creeping onto the pages of *Suits and Ladders.*

Think you can pick out the four bonehead moves I made? I will provide one half-hour of free Skype job coaching to the first 25 people who answer correctly.

Since a majority of our mentors identified public speaking skills as one of their top ten corporate survival strategies (and I happen to know a thing or two about the subject) everyone who participates will receive two pdf articles that celebrate the circle of life. 1: Creating and Delivering Effective Toasts and 2: Memorable Memorials.

To qualify for the Skype coaching and to receive your two free pdf articles simply email the titles or a description of my four bonehead moves to suzen@suzenfromstein.com. Please include the words Suzen's Career-Limiting Moves in the subject line.

So, good luck, bonne chance and I'm not hiring you if you get fired. Just kidding (no I'm not). By the way, our 102 mentors said that caffeine, carbohydrates and comedy got them through the days when even their best-laid plans gave them a headache to begin with.

Research pool

51 men and 51 women consisting of:

5 international managers from:
France (1) New Zealand (1)
South Africa (1) and
the United States (2)

They work in: financial services (2), design and construction (1), IT (1), and government (1).

10 Canadians who started their careers as consultants and then joined financial services companies (3), not for profit (NFP) organizations (3), government (2) and media (2).

Our other 87 mentors have careers in:
healthcare and education (7)
media and entertainment (9)
professional services (accounting/marketing/consulting)
  and retail (16)
financial services (17)
engineering, technology and manufacturing (18)
government and NFP organizations (20)

Our mentors titles

The numbers in the round brackets indicate how many of our mentors I interviewed with a specific title.

Assistant/Associate Director (2)
Assistant General Counsel (1)
Assistant Vice President (3)
Associate (1)
Bus. Dev. Executive (2)
Chairman (1)
Chief Communications Officer (1)
Chief Financial Officer (1)
Consultant/Senior Consultant (4)
Director (15)
Economist (1)
Editor (3)
Executive Director (5)
Executive Vice President (2)
Head of Compliance (1)
Journalist (1)
Manager/Senior Manager (15)
Marketing Head (1)
President/CEO (11)
Principal/Partner (2)
Program/Senior Program Manager (2)
Project Manager/Lead (5)
Publisher (1)
Sales Director/National Sales Dir (2)
Senior Transmission Designer (1)
Senior Vice President (2)
Vice President (16)

Top ten survival skills

Before I began my research, I assumed that men and women approached corporate survival differently, that employees who worked in unrelated sectors used different strategies to survive and that people working in North America survived differently from people working in other democratic nations.

I have since revised my thinking. My research shows that the survival strategies identified in *Suits and Ladders* are universal and transcend national borders, industries and genders. Whether you work in Canada or France, in financial services or for a NFP, there are ten things you can do right now to keep your corporate job safe.

The first chart identifies the survival strategy and the total percentage of mid-to-senior level managers who identified it. The second chart tracks gender preferences (ladies first).

Chart 1 – Top ten survival strategies

This chart identifies the survival strategy and the total percentage of mid-to-senior level managers who identified it.

Percentage of Mentors	
1. Self-awareness	91%
2. Personal reputation	91%
3. Emotional intelligence	90%
4. Other hard/soft skills	88%
5. Responding to change	86%
6. Helping others	84%
7. Knowing the business	73%
8. Networking	72%
9. Working hard	66%
10. Having/being a mentor	59%

Chart 2 – Gender preferences

This chart identifies how our 51 male and 51 female mentors ranked a particular survival skill. Overall, there were only slight differences. In two cases (Emotional intelligence – Survival Strategy 3 and Having/being a mentor – Survival Strategy 10) there was no difference. The largest gender variances were in Helping others – Survival Strategy 6 and Knowing the business - Survival Strategy 7).

	Female	Male
1. Self-awareness	47	46
2. Personal reputation	48	45
3. Emotional intelligence	46	46
4. Other hard/soft skills	44	46
5. Responding to change	43	45
6. Helping others	45	41
7. Knowing the business	35	39
8. Networking	38	35
9. Working hard	32	35
10. Having/being a mentor	30	30

Chart 3 – Two other Interesting stats

Three more of our female mentors mentioned they had a bad boss than did our male mentors and (surprise surprise) seven more of our female mentors said 'Sorry' more often than their male counterparts.

	Female	Male
Had a bad boss	14	11
Say sorry when you make a mistake	11	4

Survival strategy 1: Know yourself

Introduction

Case Study: Three strikes and you're out only applies to baseball

Nature vs. Nurture

Who are you?

Show me the money - now!

Takeaways

Introduction

"I received an offer to run a multi million dollar U.S. company. I turned it down. I never wanted to have a position where I was accountable to shareholders, unions, bankers, employees and all the other people that try to influence and change your life."

91% of our mentors consider self-awareness as their most potent survival skill. Every day, they try to be more self-aware than the day before. This helps them make more money, move faster, and get to their goals quicker.

Self-awareness is not something you do once or that you only think about if you have just entered the workforce. Even the most senior executive has to check in with his or her heart and values at least once a year.

Self-awareness allows our mentors to pinpoint why they want to be somewhere, rather than just being there. Self-awareness also puts them in touch with what is important to them as people, what turns them on as professionals, and what they need to work on, in order to continue to grow. By combining this information with market realities, they can identify and profit from careers in their employment sweet spot.

One of our mentors left a job that no longer challenged him for a position that he considered a step up. It wasn't long before he realized he was no longer doing what he loved to do. Within a year, and by mutual consent, he was restructured.

He spent the better part of the following year figuring out exactly what got his adrenaline going and his heart pumping.

It took another year before he landed his dream job. Now he has a role where he is hands-on, while he administers budgets and manages his team. Self-awareness allowed him to recover his mojo, stabilize his cash flow and improve his professional outcomes.

Although self-awareness can be extremely painful if it is forced upon you (like when you lose your job), dismantling any cockeyed views about how business works and exposing any entitlement and ego issues can be both enlightening and entertaining.

When you allocate enough time on this step, you are able to define exactly what you want and what you are prepared to do to get it. So, take a deep dive while you are still green. This may help you sidestep a lot of the pain later on.

Whether you are reactive or proactive, self-awareness helps you understand what you bring to the party. This knowledge makes it easier to both own your strengths, and comfortably talk about them in job interviews, networking events and performance reviews.

Case study: Three strikes and you're out only applies to baseball

A six-month service employee returned from holidays and was let go without any prior warning. The employee was advised that the termination was due to reorganization and, on the surface this appeared accurate because a new communications director had just been hired. The unstated reason was that there were some concerns about performance, which obviously were not discussed beforehand.

Although it may not be fair, the only thing your employer owes you is your paycheck. If you make a mistake, like the service employee in this example, you may not get a second or a third swing before you are called out.

Nature vs. nurture

"Although I was climbing the corporate ladder, and was rewarded financially, I did not find the work itself particularly satisfying. One day, I realized I couldn't care less about selling another box of cereal."

Courage and self-confidence come from knowing yourself. Look for opportunities to work with as many different people from as many diverse departments and disciplines as possible. By exposing yourself to everything and everyone, you learn what turns you on.

Play to your strengths. Let's say you have great presentation skills and love to network and travel, but hate writing reports. You are offered two roles. The first is as a Corporate Ambassador with an annual salary of $50,000 and the second is as an Analyst with an annual salary of $75,000. The Analyst job involves a lot of report writing. The benefits and the culture in both organizations are essentially the same.

Without being self-aware, you will probably jump at the job with the higher salary, a move our mentors consider a mistake. If you accept the Analyst role, you will likely earn $75,000 until you get frustrated and quit, or are fired because of your attitude or failure to deliver on your objectives. Let's face it, it's hard to perform when you hate what you are

doing or whom you are doing it with or for. The solution -
find a job where you can believe in the work.

Also our mentors suggest that you remain conscious of the
allure of "sexy" jobs. For example, in financial services, a
private equity role is often seen as a high-status position.
This is likely because it is obscenely well paid (partially
true) and outrageously interesting (not necessarily true).

In reality, only one-quarter of a private equity role is
glamorous. The other three-quarters involve research,
gathering data, analysis and report writing. Is this something
you really want to do? Do you have the skills or aptitude to
do the work? Or, if you don't have them now, are you willing
to put in the work to get them?

Who are you?

*"The reason I was so successful in my career is
that there was a good fit between my personal
values and the company values. When you
question authority, you are questioning your
employer's ethics and values. Chances are
they won't appreciate that, or you."*

Your core values and personal standards inform who you are
at work and in life. Before you join any organization and as
part of the hiring process, find out if there is a values fit.
Choose situations that are complimentary because it is
impossible to change the place. If there is a mismatch,
expect to be restructured.

Carry out your own due diligence. Is there a good values
match? Do you get excited when you think about working
there? Can you get behind the company's products or services?

Do you like and respect the people that work there? Is there room to grow? Is the role a good match with your personality?

Although big organizations usually offer more opportunities to build a wider skill set, not everyone is cut out to work for one. A healthy dose of patience is required if you want to survive in a big organization like a bank, an insurance company or a government agency.

If you aren't politically savvy and don't want to wait your turn for a promotion, it may be less frustrating to work for a smaller organization, a NFP or to pursue a freelance career.

Do you require applause every time you meet your objectives? When you are part of a team, praise for a job well done comes to the group as a whole or to the superior. Can you live with the fact that you may not receive any individual praise? Ever? Many hiring managers won't even consider a candidate who is overly ambitious or who wants to move up fast at the expense of the team.

Make your employment decisions based on today's criteria, not wishful thinking about what might happen at some point in the future. In other words, go for jobs that you are capable of doing and want to be doing, right now. Be honest about your strengths and weaknesses. Guard against believing your own press releases or thinking you are something you are not.

Can you travel? If you can't, then don't apply for jobs that involve travel. Are you willing to work the night shift or the occasional weekend? If you are a single parent and have responsibilities that require you to be home at specific times, don't apply for jobs that require this type of flexibility.

If you like the company, but not your boss, you can always transfer to a different internal department. Or, I know this is hard to swallow, you can take a demotion, as did several of our mentors, when they were realized things just weren't going to work out.

Know your principles, finances and connections and live up to them. The last thing you want is to be stuck in a job you hate because you need the money to pay the bills. Build in a financial cushion so that you aren't always chasing the next dollar. Be prepared to modify your expectations if required. Even though you deserve it, resist the temptation to spend every penny you earn.

"I'm pretty sure I don't know everything."

Feeling comfortable about asking for help seems to directly connect to your level of self-awareness. Even the most successful people need guidance, counsel and advice from others from time to time. No one will offer to help you – you have to ask. If you aren't comfortable asking for help, then there is a good chance you won't get any.

And, don't worry so much. Our mentors say that 99% of the things they worried about never happened. They also suggest you give up the idea of perfection. The world's not perfect. You're not perfect. It's crazy to expect perfect results.

We all bring a lot of emotional and historical baggage into the workplace. Mistakes will happen. Self-awareness helps you recognize the error, put it into perspective, and identify what steps you need to take in order to correct it.

Figure out if you want to make a living or if you want to dedicate your life to something bigger. To help you decide what industry suits you, ask yourself the following questions. What am I good at? What do I like to do? Thirty years from now, will I look back and be proud of what I have accomplished?

Some pieces of every job are delicious, others not so much. Focus on finding a role with a bigger slice of delicious. How do you know if you've made the right decision? Ask yourself if you would do the same job if you weren't getting paid? If your answer is, "Are you kidding me?" find a career that lets you say 'Yes!'

When you believe you have identified the right job opportunity, even if your friends think you are crazy for leaving the rent and hassle free life you have when you live at home, go for it.

If you are still unsure about what to do with the rest of your life, some independent testing may uncover occupations that are suitable for your personality type. And it is perfectly acceptable to have multiples (evaluations, not personalities). 5% of our mentors completed independent evaluations at different stages of their careers.

Our mentors survive because they found careers that match their values, personality and that they love to do. Wanting the job they have also plays a large part in keeping it.

Show me the money – now!

"My salary progression was $38,000, $26,000, $50,000, $60,000, $150,000, and $200,000. The money does come eventually."

Your degree is a means to an end. You require work experience if you want to monetize it. Although it is important to be educated, the cost of an undergraduate degree is often outrageously expensive. It may be years before you see a return on your financial investment.

If your employer doesn't place the same value on your brilliant mind as does your professor, you may never earn the high six figures salary the brochure promised. You really have to appreciate the job you have, because you don't get paid all that much in the beginning.

Get rid of the attitude that if you don't get to the top in two years, you are out of there. Even if you think of your current role as a temporary assignment, give your employer the impression that you love the role you have.

If it looks like the grass is greener on the other side it may be because there is more fertilizer over there. It takes between 18-24 months on the job before you can evaluate it fully. When you are constantly changing jobs before you have taken the time to learn your assigned role, or because you don't like the people, you can't really show off your capabilities.

Having too many employers on your resume also suggests that you are not a team player, don't fit in, and have bad hair. So watch the purple streaks, at least at the beginning. Once you get into the company and start delivering, maybe you can get away with one modest purple streak.

More than half of our mentors made a lot of lateral moves, often for no increase in pay. This is a very effective strategy, especially when you don't want to take the risk, and can use the knowledge. Challenge your own thinking, and be willing to consider all opportunities, especially those that are different from how you imagined your career path would unfold.

Be prepared to do a lot of the grunt work, especially in the beginning. You can survive these less-than-stimulating projects when you realize they are nothing more than a test. Unless you prove that you can be trusted with the less interesting assignments, you will never be given an opportunity to bite into the juicier ones.

Look at it this way. Your manager is not taking advantage of you. He or she just asked you to complete the Joe-job because they think you are competent. By doing what is asked quickly, accurately and without drama, you justify their high opinion of you.

Takeaways

Courage comes from knowing yourself.

Keep building on your strengths. If a shark stops moving through the water, it dies.

Don't take yourself so seriously. Go shopping.

If the shoe don't fit, you must quit.

Practice sparkling.

Survival strategy 2: Bigger is better

Introduction

Say 'Yes'- the ones who say 'No' are the first to go

Case Study: One for the road

Look like you fit in

Keep your personal life personal

Visibility/willingness to fail

Takeaways

Introduction

"A reputation as a hard working team player, gives you a better chance of survival or at least gives you a fighting chance at survival."

91% of our mentors believe personal reputation is extraordinarily important. If your colleagues see you as hard working and flexible that is infinitely better than if they believe you are a spoiled brat. Your ability to survive layoffs, downsizing, rightsizing and restructuring is directly linked to your reputation as a low-maintenance, highly responsive colleague.

It is within your power to make people think it is a pleasure to work with you. Never put yourself in situations for which you will be sorry or, as one mentor put it, keep your side of the street clean. You have to know that you are doing your very best, given the cards you have been dealt (remember Kenny Rogers?). When that attitude takes hold, it permeates in whatever role you have, be it entry level or SVP.

Say 'Yes' – the ones who say 'No' are the first to go

No one wants to hear, "It's not my job," or "Give it to someone else." Never put yourself in a position where you are seen as the reason the project failed. The only exception is if someone in authority asks you to do something illegal. Refuse - even if it endangers your immediate career.

If you have agreed to perform a task, and want to receive a return on your investment of time and energy, give it your all. See every second as valuable and be willing to work flat out. Hold yourself to the highest possible standards.

Just going through the motions will not keep your corporate job safe. Challenge your own complacency. Make yourself uncomfortable. Go outside your comfort zone. Bring your "A" game to work with you every day. Take things on just for the fun of it. This provides visibility and improves self-confidence.

What you did yesterday is connected to how much rope your manager, your colleagues and your family give you today. You gain trust and a longer leash, I mean rope, each time you do exactly what you said you were going to do, when you said you were going to do it. Breaking up the day by texting your boyfriend, girlfriend or bookie won't keep your corporate job safe.

Before you post anything on social media, ask if you would want a future employer to see or hear that information. People form an opinion about the kind of person you are based on the information available to them at the time.

You've probably heard the saying, "Fake it till you make it." Positive self-talk has a huge impact on how other people relate to you. If you believe you are strong, capable and confident, other people will treat you that way.

As part of managing your reputation you have to add value. Watch out for unthinkingly adding risk. If someone asks you a question and you don't have time to answer it right away, tell him or her when you will have the answer. Then, get back to them when you said you would.

Case Study: One for the road

The junior manager was working at a dream job in a government agency. Unfortunately, the manager had a few too many adult beverages at the company Christmas party. On the way home, the junior manager fell face first onto the subway platform. EMS personnel rushed to the scene. So too did the police who hauled the manager off to the city drunk tank. Because the drinks were served at a company event, human resources got involved. Now the only meetings the junior manager attends are with legal counsel, the probation officer, and Dr. Phil who is helping the junior manager work through some personal responsibility issues.

Look like you fit in

"In one of the jobs, my boss was a sloppy dresser. Since I always wore business attire, people thought he was the subordinate and I was the boss."

Looks can and do kill promising careers, Even if you don't control the meeting agenda, you can control how you act and how you look. If you want to be taken seriously, avoid showing up for work with massive amounts of cleavage or wearing track pants and flip-flops. Comb your hair and shine your shoes. If you are male, wear a tie and suit jacket to all outside meetings. Pants, too.

You really have to work harder and be better when you have a messy appearance or if you don't give a damn about who sees your body art. Regardless of your right to express yourself, if you want to keep your corporate job safe, cover your tattoos and minimize the number of visible piercings unless they are in your ears or consist of a small stone in your nose. Remove all other nose rings, safety pins and other lip and eyebrow ornaments. They only cause your colleagues to debate whether you crave attention or whether you are just plain weird. Neither is good.

Keep your personal life, personal

If you are only invested in your personal life, it is unrealistic to expect your employer to be invested in your business life. It's not a give and take. As the name implies, your personal life is personal. So, keep it that way, especially fights with boyfriends or last week's adventure when you lost your license because you were driving drunk. Neither of these scenarios will win you any friends nor influence others, except in bad ways.

Limit office chat to such boring subjects as what you are reading or studying, your wedding plans, having a baby, children, pets, vacations, new home, and your charity work.

People at work are your colleagues, not your friends. If you want companionship get a dog or participate in other corporate-appropriate activities like golf, UFC and social engineering classes.

- Don't wear your heart on your sleeve.

- Know what is appropriate to talk about in a work context and what isn't.

- Don't use your sexuality to succeed.

Although it can work out, adopt a strict, 'No affairs in the office' policy. If the relationship ends, it is very awkward for everyone. Besides, you don't want to be the subject of office gossip.

Visibility/willingness to fail

"I learned more from the things I did poorly than the things I did well."

Never assume people know more than you do because they are more senior than you. Be willing to take a risk and to develop cogent arguments about why we should change from, "We've always done it this way." Of course this assumes you understand what is high-level risk and what isn't.

If you are hidden away on the back shelf no one will know you have the better product, idea or approach. Find ways to enhance your personal profile. Do a public relations campaign for yourself. This is trickier than it sounds because you can't appear to brag or to boast. The answer: talk enthusiastically about your projects.

If you are never in the office because you are always on the road, it doesn't matter that your customers and clients love you. The people in the office don't even know you, so how can they possibly love you? If most of your time is spent outside the office make sure that your internal colleagues understand how you are helping the organization and the team. Remember, your clients don't promote you.

If you make a mistake get over it – unless they fire you for it. Try to make amends. Ask if there is something you can do and then do it. Try to explain yourself, how this happened, why it happened without playing the blame game. Don't take it personally or react emotionally.

Establish yourself as someone who is sought after for something. This adds to your credibility as a candidate and as an employee.

"I made presentations at trade shows to represent the manufacturer and to get my name out there. This led to employment in an industry I love, with a company I respect."

Takeaways

Always bring your "A" game.

Fake it till you make it.

Have consistent behaviour, consistent behaviour, consistent behaviour.

If you make a mistake get over it – unless they fire you for it.

Launch a personal PR campaign, with no attack ads.

Survival Strategy 3: Emotional Intelligence (EQ)

Introduction

Build authentic relationships
Case Study: Watch what you say
Case Study: A closed door is no guarantee of privacy

Influence people to do what you want them to do

Understand and support the boss
Case Study: Embarrass the boss at your peril
When you disagree with your manager
Case Study: Remember who signs your paycheck
Developing a good working relationship with your boss

Manage your own emotional rollercoaster
Every day is not a 'take your kids to work day'
Case Study: Watch what you write

Understand the processes, the politics and the culture
Case Study: Bull in a china shop
Avoiding unwritten taboos
Case Study: Ignorance about company policy
will not save you

Takeaways

Introduction

Almost neck and neck with Self-awareness and Personal reputation, 90% of our mentors say their Emotional Intelligence or EQ helps them keep their corporate jobs safe. A high IQ may assist; it could also hinder, especially if your colleagues find it hard to understand a word that is coming out of your mouth, or think that you are a jerk.

If you want to keep your corporate job safe, develop your EQ, especially your ability to:

1. Build authentic relationships.

2. Influence people to do what you want them to do.

3. Understand and support the boss.

4. Manage your own emotional rollercoaster.

5. Understand the processes, the politics and the culture.

1. Build authentic relationships

"The minute you focus on yourself, you give yourself permission to say and do whatever you like. Things tend to go downhill after that."

Work on relationships that are important (hint: all your relationships are important). Even when you leave the organization or the product line, you take your relationships with you.

Go out of your way to thank people who help you. Just because you are the CEO doesn't mean you are more important than anyone else. Practice humility.

Focus on getting peoples' names right and spelling them correctly. When it comes to relationships, the little things are always a big deal. You can easily damage an important relationship when you miss or overlook the details.

Be sensitive to others. Everyone, including you, is an acquired taste. If you look hard enough you can find something you have in common with everyone. Practice empathy. Ask yourself how you would feel if you were standing in the other person's shoes, especially if he or she is frightened or nervous. Unless you are the boss, in which case all bets are off, demonstrate your willingness to work with everyone.

You will probably not like everyone you work with or agree with everything they say. There are little cliques and tight friendships in every organization. It is important to get along with everyone, even if he or she is dating your ex or thinks that a tarantula is an appropriate pet for a five-year old. Be the kind of person that others feel comfortable going to, bouncing ideas off of, and trust.

If you are feeling frustrated with something or someone at work, cool it. Reserve judgment for your friends and family who are used to dealing with you.

Never give an ultimatum or, if you do, be prepared to leave the company. Many people are caught saying something that is inappropriate. As you can see from the Case Study that follows, what you say and do, can and will be used against you.

Consistency of behaviour also counts. When you go to McDonalds you know exactly what you are going to get. In business, you can't afford to confuse your boss any more than he or she already is. Keep Dr. Jekyll at home, especially if the boss expects to see Mr. Hyde.

Case Study: Watch what you say

The President invited six vice presidents to brainstorm ideas about increasing market share. All the VPs were asked to submit written ideas to a professional facilitator who would anonymously present them to the group when they met. When the team was discussing a particularly contentious strategy, one VP blurted out, "Who came up with that stupid idea?" As it turns out, the stupid idea belonged to the president. Guess what happened?

When to engage

"If it's not your business, don't get involved. By interfering with the ball when it's not your play, you irritate, anger, enrage and perhaps make an enemy out of the person who is responsible. They will go out of their way to find opportunities to repay the favour."

If you are a participant in a meeting, respect the agenda. Help move things along. If someone else raises a good point, demonstrate that you are listening. Only have a contrary point of view if it adds something helpful. Otherwise keep your mouth closed.

When you are a manager, only open your mouth if you have something that is pertinent to add, if you are directly affected, or if you are willing to champion the project. If what is being discussed is not a priority for you, or if you don't have the bandwidth, stay out of it.

Once you open your mouth, you are engaged. When you are engaged, you are expected to provide input. And it better be brilliant and appropriate. Remember, if you come up with too many ideas, people might think you have too much time on your hands.

Information is currency, be frugal. Be deferential to the people above you. Keep any derogatory comments about anything or anyone to yourself. The way you talk to people will be noticed. If someone speaks negatively about their manager, a colleague or a subordinate, it is safe to assume they probably feel it is OK to malign your reputation as well.

Don't gossip about what you learned over beers, highballs or shooters (or any other adult beverage or soft drink), or spread rumours that can come back and bite you. No matter how titillating the information, if you want your colleagues to trust you, pretend you never heard it.

Don't just send emails. Have conversations. Deal directly with people, rather than rumours of people. Your colleagues have their own jobs to do and are focused on meeting their own objectives. Help them do their jobs and chances are they will do the same for you.

Case Study: A closed door is no guarantee of privacy

A senior manager was really upset about a recent performance review and was bad-mouthing the boss, a vice president, behind closed doors. The vice president entered the outside office area and overheard the negative tirade. Almost instantly, the senior manager received a pink slip.

2. Influence people to do what you want them to do

"Remember you are working with other human beings. People quit managers not jobs."

In business, things tend to happen because of influence rather than authority. Developing rapport is the first step in getting someone to do something they don't have to do. Quite simply, people won't care about you until they think you care about them.

The first step to having influence is becoming curious about what makes people tick and then observing their body language. One of our mentors never looks at the speaker during a meeting. Instead, she focuses on her colleagues. Their body language tells her where they stand and how they feel about the information being discussed and/or the speaker. This helps her to identify probable hot buttons and likely supporters for her projects.

Educators believe that people use three primary learning styles when they consume and respond to information. Some people run a movie or see a picture in their minds (visual learners). Others rewind the tape and listen to what was said (audio learners). Still others process data by feeling, playing or working with it (kinesthetic learners).

Although everyone can and does process data using all three learning modalities, everyone has a preferred learning and communicating style. If you want to establish rapport with someone else, modify your communication to suit the listener's preferred learning style.

You might be pleasantly surprised at what you learn. Watch the assumptions about what your colleagues and subordinates are thinking, hearing or feeling. Be observant. If you are highly intuitive, great. If not, ask more open-ended questions – who, what, where, when, and why. Listen to the answers.

"When you stop listening, it's usually because you have started defending yourself."

Be open to listening to alternative points of view. There are many opinions besides your own. Acknowledge the other side of the coin. Listen without prejudice.

No matter how busy or important you are, you can't afford to just sit behind your desk with the 'Do Not Disturb' light on. Actively go out of your office/cubicle. Get some face-time with the rest of the team.

Be willing to share your opinion and to give airtime to everyone, especially the people who report to you. Besides, the best information comes from more junior people, because they are trying the hardest.

Watch bombarding someone with questions. Some people feel they are being interrogated, judged or attacked when they are asked too many questions in a row. Experts suggest that you add in some personal information after every two or three questions. That way it feels more like a conversation.

Something as simple as asking a subordinate how things are going can kick-start a useful conversation. If the person responds by saying, "I feel a little overwhelmed by the number of urgent projects on my plate," they are indicating that their favourite learning style is kinesthetic. If you respond by directing the person to a visual learning medium like an online time management webinar (visual learning modality) you will erect a wall rather than build a bridge.

Give others time to process what you are saying. Let's say you have a problem with a colleague. You might want to say something like this: "I can see you are up upset." Then, count to ten.

It takes someone four seconds to process the comment, four seconds to figure out how he or she feels about the comment and two seconds before they can speak. Honour them with your silence. Sometimes listening is all you need to do to diffuse an intense situation.

Learning basic psychology is also a worthwhile investment. It is only when you begin to see the world through your listener's eyes that you will know what words to use to develop rapport. In a large meeting or a speech, it is most effective when you use words from all three primary learning styles.

3. Understand and support the boss

"You only have one priority - to make your boss happy and to keep him or her safe."

Develop a good working relationship with your manager or get your resume ready. Businesses aren't democracies and you aren't participating in a fifty/fifty relationship.

As much as your boss cares about you, what they really care about is what you can do for them. At the end of the day, you will be judged by your ability to achieve the boss' objectives.

It doesn't really matter whether or not you like your boss. Just figure out what he or she wants, how he or she wants you to execute, and then deliver exactly that.

There are two types of bosses. There are those who will never make you look good and those who will. If you can, figure out which one hired you. If it is the former, get away from them as soon as you can. If it is the latter, count your blessings and stay focused on priority number one.

Case Study: Embarrass the boss at your peril

A director went to the scheduled performance review armed with a list of accomplishments and testimonials from scores of internal and external partners. Despite this, the director received a performance rating of 'does not meet expectations.' The director appealed the assessment. Although this didn't change the performance rating, it did embarrass the boss in front of his own boss. The director was restructured a short time later.

When you disagree with your manager

"When a direction has been decided, give the boss 100% of your support."

The boss is responsible for making the big decisions. There is no point debating an instruction unless it conflicts with something immoral or illegal. If you have an idea that is different from the boss', it is perfectly acceptable to ask, "Would you be open to… or can we try this…"

If you are being directed to do something you think is detrimental to the organization, or if you believe a particular instruction is ill advised, you only have two options - do it and fix it later, or quit.

Occasionally, you will have to follow instructions that don't make you happy. Be flexible. Some people make the mistake of digging in their heels.

Not every hill is one to die on. Too many people pick a fight with someone who is completely entrenched in his or her position. Decide whether taking a stand justifies the investment of your time and energy.

If you still feel compelled to duke it out, stop, take a few breaths and think longer and harder. Maybe it's not even your problem. Look for the Zen between making your point and acting like Buddha – it is not necessary to look like Buddha, only to act like him.

If you are going to take on the boss, make sure you have your facts straight and that you have enough ammunition and allies to put the boss down. Otherwise watch out. He or she will be gunning for you.

Remember the lyrics from that old Kenny Rogers song? You know the one that went something like this, "You got to know when to hold 'em, know when to fold 'em. Know when to walk away…" Be prepared to face the music when you don't back down.

If you treat your boss fairly and focus on priority number one, there is a high likelihood he or she will see you as a valuable team player. Remember, your boss will make mistakes too.

If your boss does something you think is insensitive or unfair, rather than harbour any ill will, tell him or her exactly how you feel and why, and in the most diplomatic way possible (and in private). You can both learn from the experience. Just be careful how difficult you make it for your employer. If you share too much or too often, watch out. Your boss doesn't have the time, the interest or the bandwidth to babysit you.

Case Study: Remember who signs your paycheck

The boss instructed the manager to send out a news release for every meeting the organization attended. The manager knew this would negatively affect both the manager's and the organization's credibility. The manager explained the impact of the instruction and proposed a compromise: a once weekly summary of the organization's activities. The boss thanked the manager for the input and reiterated the instruction; the manager ignored it. It should come as no surprise that the manager is no longer working there.

Developing a good working relationship with your boss

"Look beyond the negative. One of the most valuable lessons I learned was to focus on the positive. Now, I only present what I can do and what it's going to take to achieve that goal."

Empathize. The air in the executive boardroom is usually very thin. If you have a boss with a big ego, watch out. If you want to survive, keep your head down, and do exactly what he or she asks you to do. If you have a hysterical boss, it is a waste of time to argue. Just let him or her vent. Focus on priority number one.

There is a fine line between making the boss look good and making the boss look bad because you look good. Watch your boss' reaction to your work. If you used to get all the plum assignments and that is no longer the case, your boss may have decided you are 'difficult to work with.' Regroup and refocus on priority number one.

Have the courage to ask a lot of questions, especially in the first six months. Ask how the assigned task fits in with your role. Lack of clarity around what is expected means you can't do your job well or at all.

Good managers prefer people who are not afraid to admit when they don't understand and who aren't afraid to make mistakes, providing it isn't too big a mistake and it doesn't waste a whole bunch of time.

Figure out if what you are being asked to do has broader implications. Also, see if the task can be done less expensively or more efficiently. Companies appreciate moneysaving creativity and innovation. If you bring process improvement ideas you will be noticed. Just don't expect to be paid for them or even to get credit for them right away.

Your manager is not interested in excuses about why projects are not getting done. Just do everything humanly possibly to deliver. Then, if things don't work out, it won't be for lack of trying.

There is no excuse for not doing your job well. Unless the boss handcuffs you to your desk, stop saying it is impossible to meet your targets or you don't know how to solve the problem on your own. Become accountable for your piece of the pie. Cooperate with others to get things done, rather than complain about the roadblocks. Remember, if you aren't part of the solution than it is likely you will be seen as part of the problem. This will not keep your corporate job safe.

If there really is no way you can get all twenty projects done in the time allotted, ask your boss to pick his or her top five priorities. Deliver those – on time (a day or two earlier would be even better) and impeccably.

No matter how entertaining it is to watch the boss freak out, if there is a problem, screw up your courage and tell him or her before one small problem turns into a colossal disaster. Remember priority number one.

Say 'Yes' to assignments, especially those no one else wants to do. Saying 'Yes' develops trust and shows the boss you are reliable and a team player. You may also learn something you can use later on. One of our mentors became the go-to guy because he took minutes. Volunteering to perform this junior task exposed him to confidential aspects of the business and to members of the executive team. He flew up the corporate ladder.

A bad boss provides opportunities to learn. Respect the position, even if you don't respect the person who occupies it. In military terms, this is known as 'saluting the uniform.' If nothing else, this will keep you focused on priority number one.

Bosses have their own projects and objectives. They rarely have the time to become intimately acquainted with yours. Learn when to brief your manager and when not to bug him or her with the minutiae of your day. Always brief the boss before any client, shareholder or board meeting. He or she will love you even more if you figure out how to make them look good in front of their boss.

Believe it or not, the boss appreciates it when you take the time to acknowledge his or her efforts if they have helped or went to bat for you. It also helps the boss assess his or her effectiveness as a manager.

Should you socialize with the boss? It all depends on the chemistry. Although one of our mentors regularly slept with the boss (get your mind out of the gutter; this only happened because the two of them were on an airplane, travelling to a client site) most report that they do not make a habit of socializing or sleeping with the boss.

4. Manage your own emotional rollercoaster

"Keep your emotions at home. If you don't understand yourself, your hot buttons or what happens to you in highly emotionally charged situations, you will fail."

Have rational and impersonal business discussions and offer logical feedback. You might want to say, "I disagree with you because…" and make it black and white.

No matter how frustrating things get, no matter how upset you are, take the high road. The worst you can say is, "I was disappointed with how things turned out." Don't give in to the impulse to argue and fight. All that does is put the other person on the defensive. Maybe you will have to work together in the future.

Watch the assumptions. Until you are 100% certain that what you think is happening, is actually happening, avoid responding or even worse, reacting emotionally. In other words, never assume anything until it is proven.

Bring a positive attitude no matter the circumstances. That can overcome a lot of frustrations. Every job has moments that are a little uncomfortable. Your attitude and the way in which you execute and deliver your projects is role independent and within your control. Negativity is especially contagious. One pessimistic person can derail a whole team.

Our mentors are the same as the people who are considering hiring you. As your potential employers, they want to employ staff with can-do attitudes and who demonstrate they are capable of learning. If you have these qualities, be sure to mention them in your job interviews.

Try not to complain without a purpose or to solve a problem. Be careful to whom you vent your complaints. You don't want to have your rant used against you as did the manager in the Case Study called 'A closed door is no guarantee of privacy.' If you find yourself complaining all the time, you are in the wrong job.

Challenge yourself. Even when the task you are doing is not particularly interesting, make it a personal challenge to always find some way to make the job, the people or the environment interesting or creative.

Every day is not a 'take your kids to work day'

If you make a mistake, fix it. There is no point getting angry or reacting emotionally. If you are in a position of power, control your desire to play zero sum games. No one wins when you throw a tantrum or your weight around.

Learn your trigger points and how to control your emotions, especially when your boss or your colleagues shoot down your brilliant idea. It's about the work. Does it suck if your great idea doesn't materialize? Absolutely, but, you don't learn any less if your idea is not chosen.

How do you react to rejection? Do you withdraw or shut down? Stubbornly defend your position? Throw a tantrum? Or, maybe you just feel like crap for the rest of the day, the week or the month? If an assignment does not work out as you expected, suck it up, and move on. When you remove the emotional attachment to your work and leave your ego at home, you can give, take in and deal with negative feedback in a constructive manner.

There are many different roads that lead to the same destination and many different ways of solving a problem. Take the time to weigh the merits, detriments and consequences of all of your decisions. If you want to be a leader, you have to be calm and collected. That way, it appears as if you know what you are doing – even when you don't.

Issues are seldom black and white. Most human quarrels are linked to differences in values and beliefs. Everyone tends to admire others who validate their worldview and argue with or ignore people that don't. If, for example, you put in many extra hours, you will value this quality in your subordinates.

Never make decisions based upon fear, boredom or emotions. The only acceptable emotions in business are excitement and enthusiasm. Anger, bullying and negativity are not acceptable. Park your emotions at the door, especially when your manager is giving you hell. Accept responsibility for your part. Thank the boss for coming down hard on you. You can both learn from the mistake.

With easy access to tools like email, it's easy to respond emotionally. By all means write that angry email. Just give yourself twenty-four hours before you hit the send button. It is amazing how different things look after you've had a chance to exhale, a few drinks and a good night's sleep. Also, be extremely careful with social media and shooting from the hip. When you spout off in the digital world, everyone sees it, including recruiters.

Figure out how to self-correct in real time. Tennis players do this all the time. Imagine the mental strength and self-control it takes to corral your emotions. If tennis players can change ineffective shots in the middle of the game, so too can you.

Case Study: Watch what you write

Three colleagues were to report to a new director, who was not yet in place. All colleagues said they had no interest in the director's role. Later that same week, one of the colleagues began ordering the other two around. The more vocal colleague responded with an email that stated, "Although I am happy to help the team in any way I can, I would appreciate being asked for my help, rather than being ordered to do so." As fate would have it, the bossy colleague became the new director and the more vocal colleague received a pink slip.

5. Understand the processes, the politics and the culture

"Management will tell you what they think the corporate culture is. Don't listen to them. Talk to someone who works there. Better yet,

talk to someone who used to work there. Ask the recruiter what happened to the person who had the job before you. Talk to that person. They are probably so relieved to get out of there, they will be happy to tell you about the hidden land mines."

There is a corporate culture and there is a department culture and they are not always the same. Cultures evolve slowly when the leadership stays the same. Cultures change quickly when there is a change in leadership.

There is a huge overlap between EQ and being more politically engaged. Business is not a gentleperson's game and it can and does get ugly from time to time. If you want to succeed in a large bureaucracy you have to recognize that politics are part of the job. If you choose to ignore the politics you put yourself in harm's way.

Learn the organizational terrain and figure out who is driving the bus. Is it one person, a team, a committee, or does anyone even care? Find out how senior management views each internal department.

Identifying the movers and shakers should be easy – they are invited to all the important meetings. If you can legitimately find a way to help them be even more successful, do so. If you can't get close enough to help them, observe what they are doing and be prepared to modify what you are doing - providing it does not get in the way of priority number one. Before you rush headlong into changing everything that is wonderful about you, check in with your values. Let self-awareness be your guide.

When you ignore the politics at work you put yourself in harm's way. The only exception to this is that, if you are really good at your job, extraordinarily good, you might be able to get away with not participating in the politics. But, even if you are one of the lucky ones, you still have to know what is going on around you.

Case Study: Bull in a china shop

A consultant asked a long-term client for a job. The client said 'Yes' and asked the new employee to lead a website initiative. The first web meeting was just getting started when a junior partner threw open the door and screamed, "That's not how we do things here!" Had the consultant-turned-employee taken the time to understand the politics, this overreaction might have been prevented, and the consultant might still be working there.

Avoiding unwritten taboos

"Follow the rules of the game, especially when you are new."

If you are a new employee, be prepared to learn a completely different language. In addition to delivering good quality work, respect existing structures and processes. The corporate culture will help you identify and avoid any unwritten taboos. If you get bogged down fighting or ignoring these you will fail to accomplish your objectives or deliver on priority number one. More importantly, your colleagues will think you are a wild card and won't want to work with you.

Never cross the line in terms of expense claims or slip out early. Whatever else you do, keep your resume polished, because, senior managers occasionally use more junior staff as pawns.

If the President comes to work in a suit, even on casual Fridays, wear a suit at least a couple of times per week (but not a better fitting one). Take a look at the type of hours the firm supports. In some organizations, you are expected to go in early and stay late, even if the only thing you do is watch your boss reading the newspaper or Googling himself. Go in on weekends just to see who is there and to get some quality face-time with the higher ups.

Your job has specific hours and the company is spending money on you and relies on you to show up on time, ready, willing and able to work. Even if you've been up all night drinking with the sales guys, your boss and the rest of the team are counting on you to show up the next morning. So, be there on time and impeccably barbered. And, bring donuts. You haven't earned the right to have flexibility without a specific discussion with your manager.

Today, a lot of people want to work from home. However, few people are effective using this employment model. Before you join, understand what the company policy is regarding work at home. You have to fit into the existing environment and be willing to acknowledge when that isn't the case.

Case Study: Ignorance about company policy will not save you

A manager was on medical leave and made a career-limiting mistake by continuing to teach at a local college in the evening while on leave. One of the students worked for the same organization and spilled the beans. There was a pink slip waiting when the manager returned from medical leave. Now the manager really felt sick.

Takeaways

Learn not to react – no one cares how you feel.

Learn to ask for things in different ways.

Learn the rules of the game and follow them.

Guard against misery becoming your only transferable skill. Don't be your parents.

Everyone, including your boss, needs to be stroked. Up to a certain point.

Survival strategy 4: Other hard and soft skills

Introduction

Presentations and writing skills

Time management skills

Have fun – work that is fun gets done

Learn at least one other language

Fitness

Takeaways

Introduction

"There is nothing worse than watching someone read his or her PowerPoint slides. You shouldn't have to look at the slide to figure out what to say. You only inspire trust and confidence when you don't read your slides."

88% of the 102 mid-to-senior level managers identified presentation and public speaking skills as one of their top ten corporate survival strategies. They also said that formal public speaking training delivered an immediate and measurable return on their investment of time and money.

Presentations and writing skills

For example, becoming proficient at public speaking allows you to stand out, and to sell yourself and your ideas with confidence, clarity and credibility. Having these skills also helps you answer behaviour-type questions in job interviews.

It is impossible to have a good behaviour-type interview without good public speaking skills. The way in which you answer the interview questions or tell your story allows the hiring manager to measure your attitude towards life, liberty and the pursuit of happiness and more relevant indicators like how you think and learn, deal with problems, and respond to stress.

When you land the job, you switch from selling yourself to selling ideas, mobilizing teams, and negotiating deliverables, timelines and salary. You have to be able to articulate how your actions and activities helped your boss, and the company, meet their objectives. Good presentation and public speaking skills help you do this.

Even the best message can be lost if they is poorly delivered. See? Being able to write well is also important. It is even better if you can write and edit other people's work.

Time/project management skills

"If someone just drops in for a chat, unless he or she has scheduled a meeting with me, I get up after one minute. Then, if they don't leave my office, I do."

Learn time and project management skills. Especially in flatter organizations, you are probably managing more than one project and get to spend less time with the boss. This forces you to set priorities.

Spend at least half a day planning your week. Figure out what can realistically be accomplished in the allotted time. Get clarity on projects. Set timelines early on. Renegotiate any unrealistic deadlines. Employ discipline to stay on task.

Avoid the temptation to engage in busy work and to do the things you like to do or that are easy for you to do but do not necessarily advance your objectives. Beware of the 80/20 rule which holds that eighty per cent of your happiness and outputs comes from twenty per cent of your activities.

On important projects (aren't all of your projects important?) identify every possible bad scenario. Surprises make the boss look bad, which means you failed to focus on priority number one. When you are really well prepared you won't get blindsided.

When you are at work, work. Watch the idle chitchat and control the amount of company time you spend on Facebook.

Have fun – work that is fun gets done

"Guard against misery being your only transfer-able skill."

When you are working 10-12 hours per day it is especially important to have some fun. Make a conscious effort to be professional in terms of your social banter. When your personal values and the corporate values align you will automatically know what jokes are appropriate. When they don't, people are likely to find your zest for jest inappropriate, rude or in poor taste.

Unless you are Woody Allen, there is nothing funny in over analyzing, trying too hard, or worrying about the person next to you. Nor is it necessary to take your life or your projects so seriously. Lighten up and people will want to work with you.

Learn at least one other language

If you live and work in Ottawa, and you want a senior role, you need to speak French. Stateside, it is Spanish. Having another language allows you to participate in meetings, contribute to virtual teams and to establish rapport. You can also understand if you are being insulted not to mention ordering better in restaurants.

Fitness

Work and play hard. People will think you have more energy when you can move quickly from meeting to meeting.

Takeaways

Speak and write well in more than one language. Curse in neither.

Manage your projects and time more effectively.

Watch getting derailed by idle chitchat. Purposeful chitchat on the other hand...

Have fun.

Join the gym. It helps when you can run faster.

Survival strategy 5: Change, change, change

Introduction

Bob Dylan was right

Set improvement goals

Introduction

"Your current employer may not even be around ten years from now. If the organization survives, it is likely because it has changed which means it requires employees with different skills."

Every business faces new forces, competitors, tools, regulations and issues. According to 86% of our mentors, if you want to stay relevant, maximize your value, prolong your shelf life and keep your job safe, you have to be willing to move beyond your comfort zone, and to be relentless in terms of self-improvement.

What you learned yesterday may not apply to today. If you can't adapt, be prepared for your employer to move on without you.

If you are a member of club Gen Y, seek out the most difficult and complex situations you can possibly find. Jump into the water and start swimming. It doesn't matter if the only stroke you have mastered thus far is the doggie paddle. Be brave enough to leave the nest, free room and board, and take that job out of town. Out of country is even better.

If, on the other hand you are a member of club Gen X or older, keep challenging yourself to find new ways to add value, provide additional services and to solve problems. This makes you more valuable to your current employer, and more attractive to the next one. Only stop learning when they close the lid.

Bob Dylan was right

"Fear immobilizes people who never advance in their career. Many of my friends remained with the same firm and had lacklustre careers. I changed companies and geographical locations and had a stupendous ride."

Far too many people are scared to change jobs. Why? Nothing is permanent, not the seasons, not the reasons, and not your career path.

Business moves quickly. Management is constantly responding to crises and to changes in the external environment. Assume there is a good reason for any changes in direction. If you want to keep your corporate job safe, slap a smile on your face, and do what is being asked.

Open yourself up to changing directions and to learning how to compromise. Rather than experiencing frustration with 'on again, off again' instructions, choose to be amazed and amused that your Draft #27 looks eerily similar to your Draft #1.

Give yourself a pat on the back for having such an early grasp of the situation. Feel confident in the knowledge that everyone else just needed 26 drafts to catch up. And, if they don't, take a deep breath, and get ready for #28.

Drop the emotional connection to your work. Your job depends on how well and how quickly you respond to new instructions. If at all possible, leave what you are working on in such a way that you can pick it back up again quickly. And, be kind. Your boss has a boss he or she must please.

"Embrace any additional responsibilities you are offered. Don't expect to be paid extra for it."

Once you get in the door, internal turnover will provide many wonderful new opportunities. Become a shining example of adaptability and flexibility, which by the way, are the same characteristics you will need if you ever find yourself in a management role or in a restructuring situation.

You can't let fear control you and you can't change what the consultants say. You can however stay positive and enthusiastic. Find the discipline to focus on what you can control, like doing impeccable work and having your department function in the most efficient manner.

Set self-improvement goals

"I wanted to be a VP by the time I was 27 and a SVP by the time I was 37. I achieved both goals."

Your career is largely self-driven. If you want to advance, you have to do more than what is required. Think of your job description as informing rather than defining your role.

Less than a handful of our mentors had formal career plans. In fact, the majority described career planning as "highly overrated." That doesn't mean they didn't set goals.

At least once a year, pick something specific to improve on your list of skills and expertise. Let's say you want to improve your ability to influence people. Ask five trusted advisors about what books you should read or courses you should take to improve your competency in this area. Do not ask your mother - she thinks everything you do is already perfect.

Our mentors regularly ask themselves what their replacements would do. To ensure they stayed relevant, every so often, several even deleted their position and their department from the organization chart. Their willingness to embrace an imaginary new world order inspired them to be even more creative and relevant.

Still unsure about where to begin? Start small. Embrace change by setting goals that contribute to the business, improve your personal effectiveness, and/or raise your profile. For example,

- Sit down with a cup of coffee and research a competitor's product.

- Have coffee with a colleague in another department. Figure out how you can help each other.

- Grab a relaxing cup of coffee and research an educational course, seminar or conference that will improve your skills and provide networking opportunities.

- Invest in boxing, tap dancing, and a cat that will lower your blood pressure because your doctor thinks you drink too much coffee.

Takeaways

Expect change, and expect people to ask for it.

There is life beyond the project.

Keep your skills and your resume up to date.

Move beyond your comfort and time zones.

Set goals.

Survival strategy 6: It's not all about you

Introduction

Be the type of colleague that you would like to have

Takeaways

Introduction

*"Wherever I join a new company, the first thing
I do is to meet with my colleagues to see how I
can help and to find out what our department is
doing that drives them crazy."*

84% of our mentors advise us to focus on giving to others
and on making the lives of our subordinates and colleagues
easier. There is no limit on karma. Start giving now, even if
only for selfish reasons.

Talk to your colleagues. Real people are far more interesting
than the voices and tragedies in your head. Illusions create a
lot of fear and insecurity in yourself and others. Cultivate an
abundance mentality. It is easy to be seduced into thinking
that when I make you more successful I somehow make
myself less successful. When you are part of a team, the
opposite is true.

Each of your counterparts has their own job to do. Before
charging ahead with your project, ask yourself, who else is
likely to weigh in on this? Who can advance or slow down
my project? Reach out to them.

When you fail to consider your colleagues' objectives, you
can inadvertently become an obstacle in their world and they
will return the favour by creating an obstacle in yours, as did
the consultant-turned-employee described in the Bull in a
china shop Case Study. When you realize that your actions
will have an impact on others, you can often disarm potential
problems.

When you are a manager only take on work you can do well
and do fast – it helps if you know what that is. You can

unknowingly derail the rest of the team if they assume you are doing something you aren't doing or if you lie or inflate what you are delivering and when.

If you get your work done in the first hour, ask someone else on the team what you can do to help him or her. This is not as easy as it sounds because you can't make it look as if you have nothing to do or that the person you want to help is incompetent.

When you help out, you learn empathy, collaboration and cooperation skills. You require all of these skills when you are a manager. In other words, by helping others, you are really helping yourself.

Be the type of colleague that you would like to have

"There's a well-worn expression that goes: Be nice to people you meet on your way up because you will meet them again on your way down."

Learn as much as you can, from as many people as you can. Make time to meet with people and help them on their way up. Even if you only give them five minutes of your time, they will never forget it.

If you go to a meeting and someone shares a piece of relevant information, thank him or her, and identify exactly how you were helped. When you take the time to acknowledge how you were helped, the person that provided the help will be happy to do so again. If you neglect this step, it is unlikely the person will want to help again.

Treat everyone with respect, especially the service staff. If the receptionist or the IT guy hate your guts or think you are a pompous ass, your calls will probably be dropped every now and then, and your computer code problem will stay that way. You may even want to consider treating them better than the boss because they actually help you get your work done.

Be socially fearless. Smile and say hello to everyone on the team as well as people you don't know. Be helpful even if there is no immediate reward or if you think the task is beneath you.

When there is a tight deadline, lick envelopes, staple, copy documents, dig trenches, go on a coffee run, or do whatever else needs to be done to help out. If you insist on attending yoga class in the middle of a deadline or refuse to help because stapling and copying are not part of your job description, keep your resume handy.

Build bridges. It's just as important how you leave a job as the projects you worked on while you were there. Even when you leave, give as much notice as you possibly can, put your files in order, organize your desk, so that whoever takes over has an easy time. When you take the high road, you can continue to network with old colleagues.

Takeaways

There is no overdraft on karma. There's no line of credit either so be nice proactively.

Learn to knock on doors before kicking them down.

Have a customer service mentality.

Show gratitude.

Build bridges.

Survival strategy 7: It's Supposed To Be Hard

Learn the biz

Focus on personal growth and development

What to do when you make a mistake

Try before you buy

Takeaways

Learn the biz

"I knew something about media relations, technology, regulatory matters, capital markets and issues with a listed company. In other words, I knew four or five disciplines besides my own. This meant I could have fruitful conversations with almost everyone."

73% of our mentors say it is essential to know the business if you want to keep your job safe. When you don't understand your role, it's also impossible to recognize good and bad managers.

It takes time to learn a subject matter or to become a technical expert, to understand how your role fits in with the rest of the organization and to develop the competencies and connections that are needed to do your job well. In his book Outliers: The Story of Success author Malcolm Gladwell said that you have to put in 10,000 hours before you become a subject matter expert.

When you are a generalist you only tell someone something they already know. It is only when you are a specialist that you can add real value. You also need to know the details if you want to make correct decisions.

Internal departments in large organizations tend to be silo-ed. One department does not necessarily talk to the other (just like most marriages). Companies need people who understand other disciplines, who know what the different internal departments do to meet company objectives, as well as how to bridge any gaps between them.

Read everything you can (both online and in print). Meet other people who work in your industry. Both of these activities help you learn the industry buzzwords and understand and make sense of the conversations going on around you.

Look at the big picture. Figure out how what's going on in the external environment affects your organization and its customers, clients and suppliers. Know what the competition is doing and what people are saying. This helps you identify inefficiencies. If you want to keep your corporate job safe, you can't just say, "That's interesting" and walk away.

Even if you have just entered the work force and are not required to know this information now, you will require this information in the future. Besides, if you don't understand what's going on in the world you can easily get blindsided if the company is suddenly in trouble.

You really have to know what's going on before you can figure out what problems take the most time to fix. To turbo charge your learning, seek out senior level people and pick their brains. They will help you learn how to assess the risk/reward inherent in the different scenarios and to identify opportunities that will save the company time, money or both.

Focus on personal growth and development

"You are there to serve the organization and receive a salary for doing your job. You live in a fantasy world if you expect to be promoted if that is all you do."

To continue to grow or progress in your career, you need to grow or advance your skills and knowledge. Seize every opportunity to get new skills. When you do, you gain confidence.

Always ask yourself, "What can I do to improve what I'm doing and to move ahead? What training do I need?" Once you have the tools and know how to use them, you are a more valuable employee and a more confident individual.

Even if everything you are doing is working, think about it in a different way. No matter how brilliant your idea is, shoot it down the first time in your head. You might be pleasantly surprised at what you learn that you hadn't thought of before. Rethink and rejig your material to reflect this.

People aren't always hired for their knowledge. They are hired for their ability to learn. As you move up, you will probably be asked to do something you have never done before. That doesn't mean that you can't do it.

Before you start making decisions that can hurt you, take the time to learn everything possible about your new role, colleagues and department. If you have joined the organization in a management role, shadow more junior staff. Suck it up and spend a few days on the front desk, call centre, back office or on the assembly line or night shift.

If you have your eye on a senior management position one day, don't get yourself pigeonholed in any one function. One of our mentors spent ten years in progressively responsible operations positions. When people thought of company operations they thought of her. When she realized there was no further room for advancement, she worked her way into a business development role, even though she knew nothing about sales and marketing.

What to do when you make a mistake

"You have to be challenged to retool."

Unfortunately you need to test your assumptions and to have your solutions thrown back in your face. When you make a mistake, show remorse. Don't just say, "I'm sorry." For your apology to have any meaning, identify the lesson and what you are going to do differently next time.

There is no such thing as a perfect report or project. Get yourself and your ego out of the way long enough to critique your key projects. Figure out what went well. Identify any gaps. Pinpoint what you can improve the next time. Share what you have learned with the rest of the team.

The worst time to upgrade your skills or to retool is in the middle of a crisis or when you are forced to upgrade because your role has been restructured. Our mentors constantly upgraded their skills and made career moves that advanced them.

Try before you buy

Even if you would prefer a full time job, take that contract. You never know what contacts you will make or if the person you are replacing will even return from maternity leave.

Takeaways

Learn other disciplines.

Watch being pigeonholed in a particular role.

Focus on personal growth and development.

Show remorse when you make a mistake.

Take that contract. Hope they have quadruplets.

Survival strategy 8: Double your pleasure

Introduction

Case Study: You never know how well connected someone is or how they can help you

External networking

Nurture internal relationships

Participate in company-sponsored events

Case Study: What goes around comes around

Volunteerism

Takeaways

Introduction

"My biggest mistake was that I played the good girl card. I thought that if I worked really hard, I would get noticed. I focused more on doing a good job than on building relationships. Relationships trump everything."

72% of our mentors encourage us to network with people from all levels and from inside and outside our organizations - regardless of their age, rank or serial number. The receptionist is the most powerful person in the organization because he or she knows everyone and everything about what is going on.

Networking won't save you if you don't consistently rock your projects. However, if you want to keep your existing corporate job safe or to get a new one, it is important to build internal and external business networks and a wide variety of business friendships. It is impossible to get and keep power and influence without them.

Networking helps you expand your circle of influence. As you network, you will meet new people. Some you will learn from and some you will teach. Networking helps you expand your influence, which is why your professional relationships are one of your biggest assets. Limiting yourself to only networking with people who are immediately useful is extremely short sighted. When people in your network grow in their careers, they can help you grow in yours.

Having a good network can help you secure employment especially when you consider that only 20% of positions are filled by recruiters or through job boards. Moreover, if people with the same skill set apply for the same job, nine times out of ten, the person who is most connected, gets it. Your network is also a valuable source of advice if something goes horribly wrong.

The people you meet really want to talk about their favourite subject – themselves - and what they are thinking about and working on. Help them advance their game and they will probably be open to returning the favour.

If you have been restructured (being restructured is so common these days that people are rarely even curious about the details), your network may save you from losing what is left of your mind. They will listen and support you. They will give you contacts and contracts. Even if they refuse to lend you money, they are probably good for a cup of coffee.

Face time is essential when networking. No matter how busy you are, spend at least two hours a week having coffee dates with your peers and members of your network. You may learn something you can use in your job or you might even meet your future employer.

A word of advice: be very cautious about what you tweet, pin or post. Recruiters are watching and may veto a hiring decision if they think your communiqués are unprofessional. Use your social networks effectively, not as vehicles to spy on the competition, stalk your former boss or entertain yourself.

Case study: You never know how well connected someone is or how they can help you

The boss brought in a team of consultants to help with a high profile project. If the manager had known the extent of the bond between the boss and the external consultants the manager wouldn't have ignored the consultants quite so much. A valuable opportunity to build a business friendship with some very important and well-connected people was missed. These connections might have helped when the manager was restructured. Just because someone comes from outside your department, don't assume they can't positively (or negatively) impact your career.

External Networking

"Good relationships require time and effort."

Networking is more than handing out a business card at a social event or having hundreds (thousands?) of LinkedIn contacts and Facebook friends. It involves touching the lives of the people who touch yours, in an authentic way. People do business with people. To encourage them to do business with you, show them what's in your heart, as well as what's in your mind.

Follow your network on Twitter. Read their blogs. You may "like" what someone is doing but they won't "like" you very much if you are too busy or lazy to post a thoughtful comment. What you say doesn't have to be brilliant. It does have to be authentic. False compliments are known for what they are and people can smell a fake a mile away.

Ask yourself, "What do I have to do to touch this person's world in a meaningful way?" If, for example, you know that person is interested in organic cooking and you come across a great recipe, or read an interesting article on organic food, send it to them. Of course, this assumes you actually know they are interested in organic cooking.

Establish an authentic relationship with at least one person per month - twelve (12) people a year (whichever grows more quickly). It is also important to build your network when you are employed. Don't wait until you are unemployed and haven't spoken to someone in five years before you reach out to him or her.

Never assume even your closest associates know your skill sets, capabilities, and interests. Fully communicate what you would love to do. That way they can help you get there. Be prepared to do the same.

Nurture internal relationships

"The best advice a boss gave me was to go to the technical training course during the day. Then, go to the bar at night, because that is where the partners and trainers hang out. While everyone else is in his or her hotel room studying the technical material, I am usually the only one who is in the bar, establishing relationships and learning about future projects."

What someone else is doing has an impact on what you are doing. You just may not have made the connection yet. Hang out. Get in some face time, especially when you first join the company or move to a new department. You might be pleasantly surprised at what you can find out when people are kicking back over a few beers.

Develop a back channel with someone who is more senior than are you. When you run into issues, it is really great to have an advocate at the senior level. And you will run into issues.

Relationships with your peers can make or break your career. Your peers are your biggest fans when they like you and your worst nightmare when they don't. If there is a problem and you have fans in other departments that are also affected, you can solve it together. A lot of people get caught when something they are working on falls apart and they don't have the relationships required to resolve it effectively.

People also get into trouble when they think they know more than they actually know and boldly move ahead, without asking the right questions. Maybe what you proposed was tried before. You need to know this in advance and before you spend a whole lot of time and energy spinning your wheels or raining abuse on your colleagues. Your internal network can provide important intelligence.

Remember, there are personal friends and there are business friends. They are different. Make sure you have a decent relationship with someone before you trust him or her. Until you do, be extremely careful about what you say. There is always someone in every organization that runs to the boss with gossip.

As mentioned before, remember to include more junior people in your network – junior staff is just as terrified of screwing up as are you. And, who knows, one day he or she could become your boss, or you could be theirs.

A good internal network also gives you a talent pool to draw upon when you get promoted. Eventually you will have to hire your own stable of talent – it saves time and effort when you know people who already like and respect you.

Be open to changing the kinds of things you are doing at different points in your career. It keeps you in touch with different aspects of the world and allows your heart and humanity to keep pace with the changes in your title and salary. This instantly builds your profile.

When you become a senior manager, at least half of your networking should be focused on networking down and helping other (especially more junior) people. When you become part of the senior management team, this increases to 80%. Only twenty per cent of your networking should occur with your peers.

Participate in company-sponsored events

Even if you have too much to do and not enough time to do it in, participate in company "meet and greets." Generally the CEO is there. Have some pizza and beer and build a few relationships. Down the road, this investment of your time will pay off.

Say 'Yes' to corporate volunteer opportunities. This helps you understand the charities your company supports and why. It also gives you opportunities to network with people who will remember what you did and who may well be your future advocates.

Case Study: What goes around comes around

The executive assistant to the VP of Operations was going on vacation. She asked an associate to do her and her boss a favour by helping with his charitable projects, outside of regular office hours. The associate was happy to help.

Several months later, the associate applied for a different role in the same company. HR turned her down.

The next week, the associate and the EA bumped into each other in the lunchroom. The EA mentioned she thought of the associate when she saw the recent job posting. The associate told the EA she had already applied and that her application was unsuccessful.

The associate was gob smacked when HR called that same afternoon and offered her that position or any other position that she felt might be appropriate. Apparently the VP of Operations called his buddy, the VP of HR, and endorsed her application. This example proves why it is important to help others. Eventually, what goes around will come around.

Volunteerism

"My job defined me so much so that when I was restructured it sent me into two-years of misery and loss."

Establish connections with your community. That way you don't leave all your connections behind when you leave the job. Although volunteering makes you a better person, it won't necessarily help you become a better employee. It does however, have significant other benefits.

You get to do something really meaningful with people who have different life experiences, attitudes and ideas. Since you are required to work with them, you learn how to collaborate and to compromise to get things done. This increases your EQ and in most cases, is often more meaningful than networking over a game of golf.

Volunteerism also helps improve your management skills, develop other hard and soft skills and gain board experience. This rounds you out as a person. You may also be exposed to something that will help you do your job better, faster or more effectively. When you use this information to contribute to the business, you earn personal capital that you can spend in the future. Maybe you will have banked enough personal capital to keep your corporate job safe.

Heads up: if you are spending forty hours per week working on charitable projects, your boss and your colleagues might begin to wonder why you have so much time on your hands. Be careful to balance your participation or the poor shall be with ye always.

Takeaways

Build business friendships. Don't worry about the oxymoron.

Give heart as well as mind.

Invest in face time.

Network with everyone.

Volunteer your time.

Survival strategy 9: Performance Pressure

Introduction

Maternity leave

Takeaways

Introduction

"I demonstrated my commitment to the company by working excessive hours. It's necessary, even if it isn't fair. You have to be self-aware to know if you can live with that."

66% of our mentors work at least sixty hours and often more than ninety hours each and every week. In many cases they don't leave the office until the wee hours.

If you want to move up you can't just stand around talking to people, hanging out or watching the clock. Banish laziness. Avoid taking shortcuts and doing the bare minimum. You have to be 5-10% better than everyone else to get opportunities. You don't get promoted by going home at 4:30 p.m. and coming in at 9 a.m. It especially won't happen if you smell like a distillery.

If you want to schmooze with the executives, they get in early and stay late. When you leave early and show up late you are missing valuable social interaction time between you and the people that have the ability to promote you.

Balancing work and outside life is a nice concept. Your work is your life and that is the only balance you are likely to get. There is no way around it – you have to put in the time if you want to succeed.

As you are building your career, minimize outside distractions and focus on working hard while you are still young and free of family responsibilities. Nobody wins when you are torn between two lovers.

You don't get passed over for promotion because you worked too hard. Take opportunities when and where they arise - there are crises and opportunities everywhere. Get exposed to everything, even if it's only to verify that it is something you'd rather not do. If the job you are now in fails to increase your employability or enjoyment, leave.

If work is the only thing on your plate, eat out once in awhile. You get energy and inspiration when you balance the demands of a busy career with outside interests like sports or volunteerism.

Take drum lessons, write music, learn a new language, teach water polo, run a marathon, earn your black belt, be a Big Brother or Big Sister, or grow your own fruits and vegetables. Just do something else besides work all the time.

Maternity Leave

Although it was by no means a consensus opinion, it was raised by enough of our female mentors, that I would be remiss if I didn't include it. If you want to have children and a great career, you can't afford to take a 12+ month hiatus from your job to have your baby.

Business moves quickly. There are new projects, priorities and personnel changes all the time. Despite what the law says, your role and the business may be totally different when you return from your maternity leave.

It is recommended that you get regular updates on what the team is working on while you are on maternity leave. As soon as the baby sleeps through the night, take on special projects – don't expect to be paid for them. Attend a meeting once in awhile. This keeps you visible and connected to the team, the department and the company.

Takeaways

9-5 is a great concept.

Your work is your life. That's the only work/life balance you are likely to get.

Be 5-10% better than everyone else. Be 15% better than you were.

Measure deliverables rather than hours.

Even if you are on maternity leave, stay connected to the team.

Survival strategy 10: Mentors help you improve your technique

Introduction

Case Study: Wanting a Mentor and Having a Mentor Are Two Different Things

Takeaways

Introduction

"Early in my career, I established an unofficial advisor network. I designated five people I trusted and respected and with whom I felt I had a connection. I go to them for advice when I'm stuck on something. None of them are my personal friends or relatives, which means they don't make excuses for any of my poor choices."

59% of our mentors have confidential conversations with a web of their own mentors. Some organizations now have formal mentoring programs for their senior staff. Only one of our mentors participates in a formal mentoring program. The rest either adopted their mentors or were adopted by them.

Our mentors' mentors work for the same company, a different company, in the same industry, in another industry, or are employed in academia. They have different titles and specialties. They are different ages and genders. Friends and family make lousy mentors because they will make excuses for your bad behaviour.

Let's say you want to be an investment banker and don't have a mentor. Identify four or five people who are great investment bankers. They are usually flattered that someone sees them as wise and successful. Since they are already living your dream, you can trust their advice. They also have wide networks, can introduce you to more senior people and can often create employment opportunities for you.

Companies want to know how you will add value. There are many people that can do your job and sit in your chair. To keep your corporate job safe, you have to make a contribution beyond the job itself. Having a mentor to advise and guide you can help you avoid making any career-limiting moves. It is not a free ride. Your mentor may ask you to do a research assignment or work project for them. It's a fair exchange for saving you from making career-limiting moves.

"At the end of my six-week placement, I applied for and got a full time role with the company. I was shocked when my coworkers didn't talk to me. They would go to lunch without me. Very humbling. One of my older colleagues finally told me the team didn't really like me because I was so critical. That was my first of many lessons in corporate appropriate behaviour."

One of the things your mentor can help you with is to tell you when your behaviour is inappropriate.

None of us ask for help nearly enough. If you are a woman in business asking for help is still considered a sign of weakness. You can also be over-helped and over-coached. At some point, you have to have enough faith in your own abilities to fly solo.

Look for good people to mentor and coach. Doing so allows you to use your mind in different ways and gives you opportunities to refine your rapport, empathy, and negotiation skills. You require these skills if you want to advance.

Case Study: Wanting a mentor and having a mentor are two different things

The boss always provided nebulous instructions and was never available to answer questions. After a particularly stressful deadline, the senior manager confided in a VP the manager wanted as a mentor. The manager did not realize the boss and the potential mentor went to the same university and lived on the same street. Guess what happened? The senior manager was never mentor keep the job.

Takeaways

Seek mentors at different levels and with different ages and genders.

Internal or external – it matters not.

Listen to their advice.

Watch being over-coached and over-helped.

When you can, mentor others.

Suits and Ladders Corporate Survival Guide

General rules of engagement

The first year

Getting promoted

Takeaways

General rules of engagement

- Typically, a new CEO wants their own team. No one is safe, even those in entry-level positions. Always have an updated resume. If there is a new CEO, start shopping.

- Consistently rock your projects. The slate is wiped clean at the end of every pay period. You are at risk if all of your accomplishments are more than two weeks old.

- Be prepared with a thoughtful, focused and entertaining answer when the boss asks, "What have you done for me lately?" For example, a good answer might go something like this, "Brought off the new IPO…Made you look like a genius…Pulled a rabbit out of a hat…"

- Don't expect your boss to tell you what to do or to provide coaching on an hourly or daily basis. You are being paid to do a job, so do it.

- Learn how to deal with push back in a positive manner. You have to be able to explain what you did and why you did it.

- Only present tangible, measurable results like money saved, efficiencies achieved, etc. Unless you are the boss, avoid exaggerating your contribution or taking credit for someone else's work.

- Always return your phone calls and respond to customer queries, as if that is the only thing you have to do. There is no requirement to have 'manager' in your title before you do this.

- Always say 'Yes' when offered a new assignment, whether you want to do it or not.

- Most people are great planners, but lousy when it comes to following through. If you want to inspire trust, do what you said you were going to do, when you said you were going to do it.

- Whatever you say or do, don't piss off anyone with a higher pay scale or piss on anyone with a lower pay scale.

- Never go to a meeting where you are asking for something unless you have already gone to all the stakeholders and understood any objections and dealt with them in advance. In other words, never ask a question you don't already know the answer to.

- Always say thank you and show gratitude and appreciation to everyone in the workplace, including the boss.

- Be willing to clean up someone else's mess. Don't expect your Herculean efforts to result in a promotion or a bonus. Avoid playing the blame game or leaving a problem for someone else to clean up.

- Whether you work for the government or a private sector organization, there are a large number of processes, hoops and people to satisfy. This can lead to deceleration. Once the objective is known, the speed of achieving it is extremely important.

- Be self-motivated and have confidence in your own decisions and abilities.

- If you have changed roles, take on some kind of special project. This will give you visibility and credibility and create opportunities for you to interact and network with other people in the company.

- Identify and understand the different roles people play. Get to know your colleagues in different departments. Help them when you can.

- Constantly ask yourself, "What if…" (e.g. What if I felt less threatened and became more self-confident?). Then act 'as if' you felt less threatened and more self-confident.

- Stay focused on results. You don't have to be liked to get things done. Some people think being warm and fuzzy is more important than meeting deadlines. Don't be one of those people.

The first year

All you are doing in the first year is achieving your objectives and performing. Avoid wasting even a minute of your time worrying about whether or not you have a job. You are better off worrying about whether your boss will have a job. Remember to focus on priority number one.

Don't take on too much in the **first three months** or think about being perfect right away. Be prepared to take orders (take detailed notes, too). Be punctual.

Learn your employer's mission statement, vision and values because they tell you how to behave. If the company slogan calls for customers for life, then do everything in your power to make sure your customers stay committed to you.

Ask your boss how you can succeed. Speak up if you don't know when or what you have to deliver. Get to know the boss as a person and learn how he or she works. Understand what is expected of you and clarify your key objectives.

When you understand what your boss wants, layer in the company philosophy and deliver what is asked you develop trust. With trust comes opportunity, including more responsibility, more creative assignments and more leverage, especially when your boss knows he or she can count on you to deliver.

Remember, you are in the learning and observing mode. People expect you to ask a lot of questions. At the end of **six months** however, you are no longer the 'new kid' and are expected to know what you are doing.

Never overpromise, under-deliver or lie. Your boss doesn't want to hear excuses about why things aren't done. And, they don't want any creative input from you for the first six months, either. They just want you to execute. Spell-check everything.

Not all companies have regular performance reviews. Regardless of the policy, talk about your performance with your boss at least once every six months. Find out if he or she is happy with what you are doing. Confirm that you are meeting your objectives. Ask if there is something you can do to improve your results.

Our mentors acknowledge there is a lot of negative press around the work ethic of Gen Y largely because so many of its youthful representatives appear to be more interested in chilling with their buddies than in working for the Man.

If the only questions you ask in your job interview is when you can get benefits, when can you have flexible hours and when can you work from home, there is a good chance you will not be the successful candidate.

However, this laissez faire attitude towards work provides

many wonderful opportunities for people who want to earn enough money to pay their landlord, their student loans and eat dinner out once in awhile. Be sure to stress your willingness to work hard in your interviews.

Even if you are happy in your current role, if asked about your future plans say, "I want to explore all opportunities." Companies want employees with aspirations. If you don't have any, senior management won't trust you. And when they don't trust you, you are at risk of being fired. Contrary to popular belief, you are most vulnerable when you hide in the perceived safety of your own department or just do your job.

Climbing the Corporate Ladder

"I changed jobs every two to three years. In the first year I was training. In the second year I was delivering. By the third year I was getting bored and looking for the next challenge."

Be committed and be loyal, but not so blind or so loyal that you overlook other opportunities. When warranted, ask for opportunities to advance – don't wait for your boss to promote you or to know what you want to do.

Be very specific. If, for example, you want to travel and take on foreign assignments, make your aspirations known. Clearly communicate what you bring to the table and why you deserve the opportunity. In the early days, one of our mentors felt her colleagues were smarter and more worthy of the money and the promotion than she was. She did not start to climb the corporate ladder until she acknowledged that her self-limiting beliefs were holding her back.

Observe the people who get promoted. Figure out what they are doing. Emulate them. It is important to be with an organization that gives you opportunities to grow. Have some idea about how long it should take to move up before you ask for the promotion or the raise. Unless they expand the role, don't stay in any place too long.

If you aren't promoted in four to five years, move on. Regardless of how comfortable you are in your current role, change every two to five years. You can stay with the same company, just join a completely different department.

Read the job ads for the next level up. Figure out the academic qualifications and work experiences you need if you want to be considered a good candidate. Follow people in your company, your industry and on LinkedIn who are doing the job you would like to do. Shadow them (stalking them is not recommended). Do what they do.

Figure out how to train others to do your job. Being too good at any one thing is extremely risky. Management will be reluctant to promote you if you are the only one who can do your job.

Remember to focus on priority number one. That way your boss may take you with them when they move up or move on. A number of our mentors worked for the same boss at different companies.

Avoid saying 'No' to a new role, a new department or a physical move more than once. But, as you move up, learn to be discriminating about the projects you take on. People will continue to heap more stuff on you if you say 'Yes' to everything. This may compromise your ability to deliver on your objectives.

As you move up, your role changes from doing the work yourself, to managing others who do the work for you. Are you willing to give up doing the work yourself and to rely on staff to do what you asked? If not, don't count on being promoted any time soon.

As you climb the corporate ladder, your responsibilities, budget and number of people reporting to you become more costly. Your employer won't take a chance on you unless they trust you.

Learn about financial management. When you appreciate the general financial picture, are fiscally responsible, and know how to put together a budget, you develop trust with senior management. You will likely be offered bigger responsibilities and will be considered, or be next in line, for a position when it comes up.

Takeaways

There is a clean slate every two weeks. Then, get your hands dirty again.

Ask lots of questions.

Ask for opportunities to advance.

Train others to do your job.

Learn financial management. Don't be frightened. It's wild but it can be tamed, unlike many of the people you work with.

Food for thought

**Some additional advice from the
102 real people with real jobs.**

- Only follow the rabbit if you trust him or her.

- Be real.

- Choose a profession that matches your personality.

- Every day, remind yourself how lucky you are to have a job.

- Don't hold yourself back because you are scared.

- Your dream job won't land in your lap.

- Don't apply for a job you don't want to do.

- Find your X on the map and go for it.

- You don't have to be the most interesting or the quickest to succeed.

- Money isn't everything.

- Avoid the temptation to overrate your abilities.

- You are 100% responsible for yourself.

- You will not be right 100% of the time.

- Not everyone is management material.

- Always plan on being fired.

- It's better to leave before overstaying your welcome.

- Recognize when it's not working.

- You have to have a lousy job to appreciate a good one.

- Don't mess with your integrity.

- Make others look good.

- Be willing to say "I'm sorry."

- Always hire better than yourself.

- Manage up, down and sideways.
- Want flexibility? Be flexible.
- Learn when to push and when to pull.
- Ask yourself, "How important will this be six months from now?"
- Learn how to juggle.
- Let others say you are fantastic.
- Get comfortable with saying "I don't know."
- There is life beyond the project.
- Be the consummate professional.

Mentors reading list

If the 102 real people with real jobs mentioned a book that inspired or helped them, it is listed here:

30 Ways to Better Days How to Rally After You've Been Dumped by Caird Urquhart

Briefcase Moms by Lisa Martin

First Break all the Rules by Marcus Buckingham & Curt Coffman

In Search of Excellence by Tom Peters & Robert H. Waterman Jr.

Liar's Poker by Michael Lewis

Lynchpin by Seth Godin

Never Eat Alone by Keith Ferrazzi

Outliers by Malcolm Gladwell

Power by Jeffrey Pfeffer

Stop Acting Rich by Thomas J. Stanley

The Artist's Way at Work: Riding the Dragon by Julia Cameron, Mark Bryan & Catherine A. Allen

The Effective Executive by Peter Drucker

The Power of Now by Eckart Tolle

The Secret Handshake: Mastering the Politics of the Inner Business Circle by K. Reardon

The World is Flat by Thomas Friedman

Think and Grow Rich by Napoleon Hill

Thinking Fast & Slow by Daniel Kahneman

What Color is Your Parachute? by Richard N. Bolles

Working With Emotional Intelligence by Daniel Goldstein

Bonus Article

by Suzen Fromstein "Can a consultant successfully transition into employment?" originally published in Marketing Canada, The Canadian Institute of Marketing's quarterly journal, November 2012

Can a consultant successfully transition into employment?

In challenging economic times or because of changes in personal circumstances, an increasing number of consultants want to become employees. However, the strategies and characteristics that helped you survive as a consultant are not necessarily the same as those required by an employee.

I decided to talk to one hundred mid-to-senior managers from different industries and to find out what they did to survive and thrive in the corporate jungle. At the time of publishing this article, I was close to 85% through my research. Ten of the 85 people I have interviewed so far were consultants before they became employees.

Overview of Research

Without exception, the consultants-turned-employees confirmed there is a big difference between the two roles. As a consultant, you are a lone wolf and an outsider. As an employee, you are part of the pack and as such, part of the family. Behaviours that are appreciated when you are outside (and for which you may have been hired) are not acceptable once you join the pack. If you are unwilling or unable to adapt, you will not survive.

As a consultant, when the project is complete, there is no requirement to work with a difficult client again. You can simply walk away. However, as a member of the corporate pack, you may be required to work with an incompetent, rude or egotistical individual on a daily basis. If you need the job, walking away is not an option.

More than hard technical skills are required to hold onto your job. To survive and thrive, you must also develop a plethora of soft skills, including patience, communication, presentation, sales, rapport building, networking and (authentic) empathy skills.

For example, the ten consultants-turned-employees believe that it should not be obvious that you like working with someone or you don't - everyone (including you) is an acquired taste. More importantly, to fit in with the pack you have to respect the position even if you don't respect the person in it. This can be especially challenging for transitioning consultants, especially when you can do your superior's job in your sleep.

Three Success Strategies

The consultants-turned-employees consistently identified three main success strategies:

Strategy 1: Develop your hard and soft skills.

You may be hired for your hard skills such as your technical expertise or because you are a subject matter expert. Your success as an employee however, depends on your soft skills. Soft skills most consultants already have include:

- Loving change and adapting to numerous, even hourly, changes in direction.

- Leaving your ego and your expectations at home.
Not taking negative feedback personally.

- Asking numerous open-ended questions to find out
what's really happening and probing for the hidden
agenda.

- Adhering to schedules and budgets and renegotiating
unrealistic deadlines.

- Being prepared to say no if you are asked to do
something illegal or unethical.

- Having excellent writing, presentation, negotiation and
sales skills.

However, many consultants find the following list of soft
skills more challenging:

- Playing nicely with others, especially with a boss you
don't respect.

- Making decisions too quickly. Corporate decision-
making moves much slower and involves consensus
building.

- Taking risks – but not at anyone else's expense. As a
consultant you only had to think about your own actions.
As a member of the pack you have to consider how your
actions impact others.

- Interfering with the ball when it's not your play. You
have to subvert your natural inclination to do everything.

- Avoiding the temptation to work 7 days a week,
52 weeks a year.

- Saying "I'm sorry" - out loud, not in your head or
an email.

- Articulating your value – don't wait for someone else to
notice your contribution.

- Being passionate – it helps you get thru the BS!

- Having patience. Organizations change so quickly that if you lay low and bide your time, the jerk will eventually move on.

Strategy 2: Adopt a flexible work schedule and compensation model

Be open to alternative compensation models. For example, be willing to work on contract – the ten consultants-turned-employees I interviewed all started out this way. Perhaps the graveyard shift offers the work/life balance you crave. Or maybe your future employer will allow you to hold onto some of your existing clients. If so, you can probably live with a lower base salary.

Strategy 3: Manage up, down and sideways

Rather than having one strong relationship with the client representative, as an employee, you have to manage relationships at different levels of the organization. It goes without saying that you have to keep your boss informed. However, relationships with your colleagues and more junior staff can be just as important. For example, one of the people I interviewed said that they talked to the corporate librarian if they wanted to find out what was really happening on a certain project as well as the clerk on the 3rd floor, because he controlled the vacation schedule.

In Conclusion

If you aren't put off by any of the foregoing, maybe you have what it takes to fit in with the rest of the pack. The good news is that consultants interested in transitioning into full-time employment have the hard skills and many of the soft skills needed to succeed. Remember to stress both in your job interviews - this will separate you from the other 250 qualified consultants also vying for the same position.

When you have landed your new position, look around for opportunities to stand out. My research suggests organizations are always looking for people who are willing to lead a new project or a new initiative where the outcome is unknown. Most career employees are not willing to venture away from the security of their existing mandate or to take on the unknown. For example, one of the people I interviewed ended up heading a division in Bulgaria because he was the only employee willing to take on the initial six-month contract.

In conclusion, doing a good job is not good enough to keep it. To survive, you have to be prepared to refine any problem area soft skills, be flexible around compensation and be willing to develop relationships in all levels of the organization.

Suzen Fromstein's Bio

Suits and Ladders: Ten Proven Ways to Keep Your Job Safe (with a few jokes thrown in) is Suzen Fromstein's debut e-book. Suzen interviewed 102 mid-to-senior level managers (51 men and 51 women) and consolidated their wisdom into one informative, easy to read, entertaining survival guide. Her second self published e-book: Want To Inform, Influence And Entertain Like A Pro? Simply Recognize the Seven Deadly Sins of Public Speaking And Then Avoid Them is now available for purchase.

Forever the optimist, Suzen swears Killers, Coffins & Cadavers, a comedy e-book on death and dying co-authored with standup comic Michael Nemiroff and comedic actress Elaine Smookler will be published at some point - whether in this lifetime or the next remains to be seen. Until then she will continue to speak and write about more mundane subjects like career, relationships and the rapport-building power of laughter.

Prior to embarking upon her speaking and writing career, Suzen was the Director of Communications at The Investment Funds Institute of Canada (IFIC), the mutual fund industry's trade association and taught business presentations skills at a local community college.

Before entering corporate life, Suzen owned and operated The Write Connections Inc. and worked with such notable organizations as ABN Amro, Colliers International, BMW Canada, Desjardins Financial Security, Fidelity Investments and The Canadian Marketing Association.

Suzen lives in Toronto, Ontario, Canada with her cat Nikki.

www.ingramcontent.com/pod-product-compliance
Lightning Source LLC
Chambersburg PA
CBHW060047210326
41520CB00009B/1303